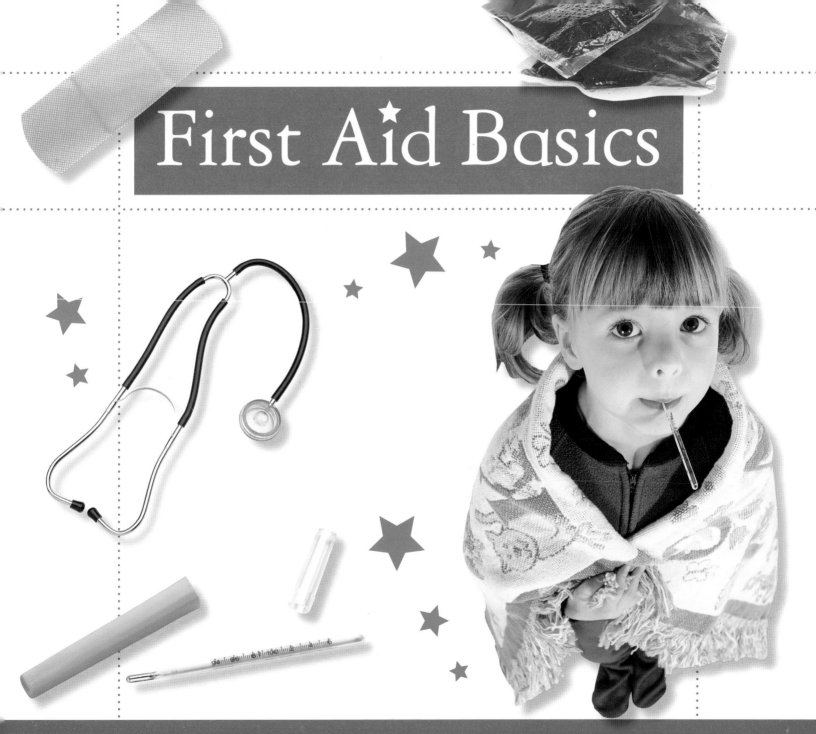

First Aid Basics

BY ELIZABETH LANG

The Child's World

Published by The Child's World®
1980 Lookout Drive • Mankato, MN 56003-1705
800-599-READ • www.childsworld.com

Acknowledgments
The Child's World®: Mary Berendes, Publishing Director
Red Line Editorial: Editorial direction
The Design Lab: Design
Amnet: Production
Photographs ©: Front cover: serasker/iStockPhoto; Comstock; PhotoDisc;
jane/iStockPhoto; Comstock, 3, 4; PhotoDisc, 5, 21; gorillaimages/
Shutterstock Images, 7; BrandX Images, 9, 16, 21; Eric Isselee/
Shutterstock, 10; Kids in Motion, 14, 19; auremar/Shutterstock Images, 13;
Suzanne Tucker/Shutterstock Images, 18

ISBN: 978-1623235376
LCCN: 2013931382

Printed in the United States of America
Mankato, MN
July, 2013
PA02174

ABOUT THE AUTHOR

Elizabeth Lang is a writer, artist, and
teacher. She lives in Olympia, Washington,
with her husband, three children, three cats,
two dogs, and a great deal of rain.

Table of Contents

CHAPTER ONE

What Is First Aid?

▶ Opposite page: Emergency medical technicians respond to 911 calls.

▼ *Sports are fun but can lead to accidents.*

There you are, riding your skateboard, and you do not see the curb. "Ouch!" Your baby sister swallows a dime. "Yikes!" Your friend steps on a thumbtack with bare feet. "Yeow!"

We try to be safe, but accidents happen. If you do not want to get hurt, you could wear a body suit made of thick steel. But you would have to wear it all day, every day. Then you would walk funny. And what if you had an itch? It is much better to be ready if and when an accident happens.

First aid is emergency care for someone who is injured or ill. You give first aid before an injured

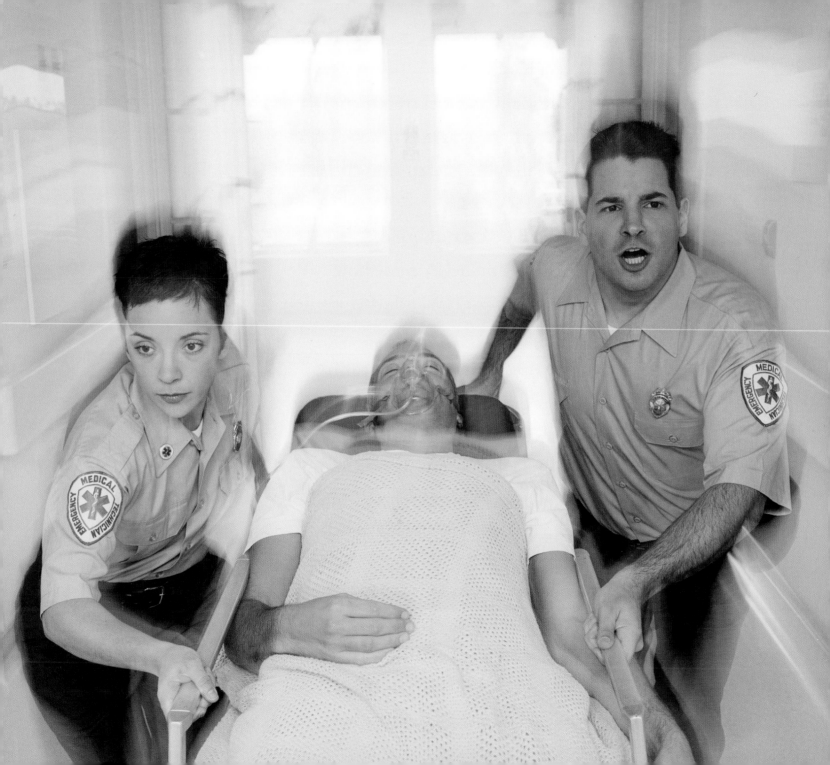

person can get professional medical treatment. If you see someone who is hurt, you might have to give first aid. This means you need to stay calm and try to remember these four tips:

1. **Call for Help**. Find an adult if one is nearby. He or she can help decide how serious the situation is. If no adult is nearby, call 911.

2. **Prepare for the Worst**. It is better to believe an injury is serious rather than take it lightly. That way, you are sure to get the person the help he or she needs.

3. **Do No Harm**. If the injury looks serious, do not try to move the injured person. Keep him or her calm and relaxed, which will help both of you. Try to keep the injured person warm and comfortable.

911!

It is not always clear when a situation is an emergency. This book will give you examples of when to call 911. In any type of emergency, the steps for calling 911 are the same:

1. Pick up the phone and press 9-1-1.
2. Say: "This is an emergency!"
3. Be ready to tell the 911 operator what the emergency is, who you are, what happened, where it happened, and when it happened.

4. **Keep Yourself Safe**. If the scene of the accident is dangerous, do not try to help the injured person. Remember to call 911 so professional medical teams come to help.

▶ *Adults can help bandage cuts and scrapes.*

CHAPTER TWO

Stings and Bites

Stings and bites can be annoying and painful. While you can treat some stings and bites at home, others need a doctor's care.

Insect Stings and Bites

Most insect stings and bites only make you itchy. Maybe you will have only some **swelling** or redness. Sometimes, people can have dangerous reactions to an insect sting or bite. The venom from bees, wasps, hornets, yellow jackets, scorpions, and some spiders can cause dangerous reactions. Bites from these insects may cause serious **symptoms**. If someone is experiencing swelling in the face or difficulty breathing, call 911 right away. Other

▶ *Opposite page: You may get a bug bite or bee sting when you spend time outside.*

potentially serious symptoms include hives, bumps, or patches on the skin that look like a red, itchy rash.

Here's what you can do to treat mild insect stings and bites:

1. If it is a sting, remove the stinger first.
2. Wash the area that was stung or bitten with soap and water.
3. Then, apply a cold pack to reduce swelling and pain.
4. Be sure to tell an adult who can keep an eye on the sting or bite to make sure it does not get worse.

Animal Bites

Animals might bite when they are teased, when they are surprised, or as a last resort because they feel threatened. Pets bite more than wild

▼ Bared teeth are a sign that a dog feels threatened.

animals do, and dogs bite more than cats. A dog often tries to warn people to stay away, but not everyone gets the message. Tell an adult any time a dog or other animal bites a person.

Sometimes, a bite does not break the skin and can be treated at home. If a bite does break the skin, it is important to go to the doctor to prevent **infection**. A bite might be infected if it looks red or is bleeding and swelling.

Here's what you can do to treat minor bites that don't break the skin:

1. Wash the area that was bitten with soap and water.
2. Next, put a dab of **antibiotic** cream on the area.
3. Then, cover it with a bandage.

CHAPTER THREE

Cuts, Scrapes, and Burns

Cuts, scrapes, and burns are skin injuries. Many cuts, scrapes, and burns are minor and you can treat them yourself. Others are more serious and must be seen by a doctor.

Cuts and Scrapes

Most cuts and scrapes are easy to treat. Small cuts and scrapes can be treated at home. But some cuts and scrapes are not so easy to treat and might need stitches or a doctor's care. If the cut is bleeding heavily or blood is squirting from it, call 911. If a cut or scrape is deep or dirty, tell

▶ *Opposite page: Keep cuts covered to avoid infection.*

an adult immediately. A cut or scrape might be dirty if it has bits of grass, metal, or dirt trapped inside it.

Here's what you can do to treat minor cuts and scrapes:

1. First, wrap a clean cloth around the wound and press firmly on it to stop the bleeding.
2. Then, wash both cuts and scrapes with soap and water.
3. Put a dab of antibiotic cream on the wound.
4. Cover cuts with a bandage, but leave scrapes uncovered to prevent infection.

Burns

Burns are injuries to **tissues**. Heat, flame, chemicals, **friction**, or the sun can cause burns.

▼ *Falling off your scooter could cause a friction burn.*

Minor burns can cause redness, swelling, pain, and even a bubble-like swelling called a blister. These types of burns can be treated at home. More serious burns require medical attention. Call 911 if burns cover a large area of someone's body or if they are making it hard for the person to breathe. Also call 911 if you think the burned person has inhaled smoke, which might happen if he or she was burned in a fire. Serious burns are best left for medical professionals to treat.

Here's what you can do to treat minor burns:

1. First, cool the skin by running the burn under cool water for 20 minutes.
2. Then, if there are blisters, gently wrap the skin with a clean cloth.
3. Do not pop the blisters as the burn heals.

CHAPTER FOUR

Splinters, Sprains, and Fractures

▼ *Sometimes, you'll need a magnifying glass to see a splinter.*

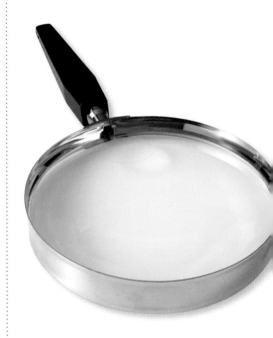

Ouch! Splinters, sprains, and fractures can be painful and may require a doctor's care. When these injuries happen, it is important to know what to do.

Splinters

A splinter can be a small piece of wood, glass, or other object that slips under your skin. Tell an adult if you have redness, swelling, or if the splinter is near your eye. To treat a splinter, you need to remove the small piece of wood, glass, or other object that is stuck. Sit in good light and grab a magnifying glass so you can easily see the splinter.

Here's what you can do to treat a splinter:

1. If your splinter is below the skin, try soaking the area in warm water for ten minutes to bring the object to the surface.

2. Then, find a pair of tweezers, rubbing alcohol, soap, and water. Clean the tweezers with the rubbing alcohol and wash your hands with the soap and water.

3. Grip the part of the splinter sticking out of your skin with the tweezers and pull.

4. After the splinter is out, gently squeeze the wound to make it bleed. Bleeding will help wash out germs.

5. Wash the area again and gently pat it dry.

6. Finally, apply antibiotic cream to the area where the splinter was.

RICE IS NICE

Rest the injured area.

Ice the injury for 15 minutes, but do not put the ice directly onto your skin. Instead, wrap the ice in a towel or use a cold pack.

Compress the injury. This means firmly wrap the injured area with an elastic bandage. Compressing reduces pain caused by swelling.

Elevate, or raise, the injured area above your heart. This helps with swelling by draining fluid from the tissues.

◄ *Opposite page: Spraining or breaking your arm may make you miss some games and practices.*

► *With RICE, you'll be healed and dancing again in no time!*

Sprains and Fractures

Limbs and bones can be sprained and broken. A sprain happens when a **ligament** has been stretched too far or has been torn. If a person can move the limb, but it is getting puffy and sore, he or she might have a sprain. Sprains are best treated with RICE: rest, ice, compress, elevate.

A broken bone is called a fracture. A person may have a broken bone if you hear a popping sound after an accident or if the person cannot move the area you think is broken. If you suspect a fracture, even if you cannot see the broken bone, do not touch the limb. Instead, call 911 and find an adult.

Hands-on Activity: Make Your Own First Aid Kit

What You'll Need:

A box with a lid, red and white construction paper, scissors, glue, first aid supplies (for example: Band-Aids, tweezers, antibiotic cream, gauze pads, alcohol wipes, an elastic bandage, cotton balls, an instant cold pack, and a small flashlight)

Directions:

1. First, make a cross with the red construction paper and a rectangle with the white construction paper.
2. Then, glue the red cross on the white rectangle—that's the symbol for first aid.
3. Next, glue the symbol onto the box. Fill the box with the first aid supplies and you're done!

FIRST AID
KIT

Glossary

antibiotic (an-tee-bi-OT-ik): An antibiotic is a substance that slows down or destroys bacteria or other organisms that make people sick. Antibiotic cream has this substance in it.

first aid (furst ayd): First aid is emergency care given to someone before he or she can be treated by medical professionals. Anyone can give first aid to an injured person, but it's always a good idea to find an adult first.

friction (FRIK-shun): Friction is the resistance that occurs when two surfaces rub together. Friction can cause scrapes and burns.

infection (in-FEK-shun): An infection occurs when germs get into your body and multiply. Your body fights off these germs with special cells.

ligament (LIG-uh-mint): A ligament is a band of tissue that connects bones together and holds organs in place. A ligament can be stretched too far or can be torn, causing a sprain.

limbs (limz): Limbs are the arms or legs of a human. Fractures can happen to your limbs, including an arm or a leg.

rabies (RAY-beez): Rabies is a disease in animals that can be passed to humans through a bite. Animals with rabies might drool, stumble, be aggressive, or behave in a strange way.

swelling (SWEL-ing): Swelling is an enlargement of a body part or tissue caused by a buildup of fluid in the tissues. Many types of injuries can cause swelling, including stings, bites, cuts, scrapes, and fractures.

symptoms (SIMP-tumz): Symptoms are changes in your body from an illness or injury. Symptoms are like clues in a mystery— they help you figure out what is making you sick.

tissues (TISH-yooz): Tissues are made up of groups of cells that do the same thing in your body. Burns and sprains can injure tissues.

To Learn More

BOOKS

Gale, Karen Buhler. *The Kid's Guide to First Aid*. Charlotte, VT: Williamson Publishing Company, 2002.

Silverstein, Alvin, Virginia Silverstein, and Laura Silverstein Nunn. *Cuts, Scrapes, Scabs, and Scars*. New York: Franklin Watts, 1999.

WEB SITES

Visit our Web site for links about first aid: **childsworld.com/links**

Note to Parents, Teachers, and Librarians: We routinely verify our Web links to make sure they are safe and active sites. So encourage your readers to check them out!

Index